MW00399286

CONFESSING THE FAITH

THE 1689 BAPTIST CONFESSION FOR THE 21ST CENTURY

Founders Press

Committed to historic Baptist principles
Cape Coral, Florida

Published by

Founders Press

Committed to historic Baptist principles

P.O. Box 150931 • Cape Coral, FL 33915
Phone (239) 772–1400 • Fax: (239) 772–1140
Electronic Mail: founders@founders.org
Website: http://www.founders.org

©2012 Founders Press
Second Printing, 2013

Printed in the United States of America

ISBN: 978–0–9849498–5–4

All rights reserved. No part of this publication may be reproduced, stored
in a retrieval system or transmitted in any form by any means, electronic,
mechanical, photocopy, recording or otherwise, without prior permission
of the publisher, except as provided by USA copyright law.

CONTENTS

3

FOREWORD

Historically, Baptists have been, and thankfully many still are, a confessional people. Yes, they are supremely a people of the Book, the Holy Scriptures. But confessions have been central to their experience of the Christian life. The twentieth-century attempt to explain Baptist life and thought primarily in terms of soul-liberty seriously skews the evidence. Of course, freedom from external coercion has always been a major concern of Baptist apologetics. But up until the twentieth century, this emphasis has generally never been at the expense of a clear and explicit confessionalism.

Of the many confessions of faith that Baptists have produced—and they have produced a goodly number—none has been more influential than the *Second London Confession*, popularly known as the *1689 Confession*. It was not only the confession of faith adopted by the majority of Baptists in the British Isles and Ireland from the seventeenth to the nineteenth centuries, but it was also the major confessional document on the American Baptist scene, where it was known as the *Philadelphia Confession of Faith* (1742) and which added an article on the laying on of hands and also one on the singing of psalms, hymns, and spiritual songs. Among Southern Baptists this confession played an influential role as *The Charleston Confession* (1767),[1] which became the basis of the *Abstract of Principles*, the statement of faith of The Southern Baptist Theological Seminary that was drawn up in 1858 by Basil Manly, Jr. (1825–1892).[2]

The truths that this confession promoted fell out of favor for much of the twentieth century, but in the last fifty years there has been a great recovery of gospel truth among Evangelicals and once

---

[1] The sole area of difference between the *Philadelphia Confession* and the *Charleston Confession* was the latter's omission of the article on the laying on of hands. The 1767 *Charleston Confession* was reprinted in 1813, 1831, and 1850.

[2] For details of the links between the *Charleston Confession* and the *Abstract of Principles*, see Michael A.G. Haykin, Roger D. Duke and A. James Fuller, *Soldiers of Christ: Selections from the Writings of Basil Manly, Sr., & Basil Manly, Jr.* (Cape Coral, FL: Founders Press, 2009), 36–40.

again there are those deeply committed to the doctrines of this confession. The English language, however, has changed over time, and
just as there are phrases in the Authorized Version (1611), also known
as the King James Version, that are no longer as clear as they once
were due to linguistic change, so it is the case with the *1689 Confession*. For this reason, this new rendition of the confession by Dr.
Reeves is indeed welcome. He has sought to render it readable by
the typical twenty-first-century Christian reader, but with minimal
change and without sacrificing any of the riches of the original text.
I believe he has succeeded admirably in both of these aims. With
confidence, then, we can say of this version of the *1689 Confession*
what the Victorian preacher C.H. Spurgeon (1834–1892) once said
with regard to the confession when he had it republished in 1855:

> This little volume is not issued as an authoritative rule, or code of
> faith, whereby you are to be fettered, but as an assistance to you
> in controversy, a confirmation in faith, and a means of edification
> in righteousness. ... Cleave fast to the Word of God which is here
> mapped out for you.[3]

Michael A.G. Haykin
Dundas, Ontario

---

[3] Cited in the "Foreword" to *The Baptist Confession of Faith with
Scripture Proofs* (Choteau, MT: Gospel Mission, n.d.), 6.

INTRODUCTION

Those of us who love the *1689 Confession* love it because we love the Scriptures. Far from denying or competing with the authority of Scripture, a historic biblical confession such as the *1689* actually promotes and confirms the Scriptures as our final authority. If there is any doubt in our minds, the confession removes it in the very first line: "The Holy Scripture is the only sufficient, certain, and infallible rule of all saving knowledge, faith, and obedience." But the confession affirms more than the authority of Scripture. It affirms that these authoritative Scriptures actually teach specific doctrines. The authoritative Scriptures will do us no good if we cannot say what they actually teach. The confession expresses the conviction that the Scriptures deliver to us a coherent, life-altering body of teaching—the *faith* (Jude 3).

Pastors are called to preach the Word—to restate, interpret and apply God's Word—and not merely to read it. A creed or confession of faith is little different from a sermon in this sense. It is a restatement of the Word for a particular purpose—in this case to summarize the overall teaching of that Word on various topics. To the degree that it expresses the doctrines of Scripture accurately, it is an expression of the Word just as accurate preaching is said to be an expression of the Word (2 Timothy 4:2). In fact, the impulse to compose confessions of faith finds biblical encouragement by the example of brief confessions quoted in Scripture itself (1 Corinthians 15:3ff; Ephesians 4:4–6; 1 Timothy 3:16). Though similar to a sermon in one sense, a confession has at least one important difference. It is usually produced by many godly minds deliberating over a long period, and it has been further reviewed and accepted by a group of churches. As a result, a confession is often more precisely crafted and more thoroughly examined for accuracy than an individual sermon.

A confession is a tried and true teaching tool. It lays out the faith in a clear, systematic way and shows the connections among doctrines. It also serves as a standard by which teaching in the church can be measured. An overseer "must be able to give instruction in sound doctrine" (Titus 1:9), and a deacon "must hold the mystery of the faith with a clear conscience" (1 Timothy 3:9). Hearing an officer merely quote the Bible does not tell us whether he understands the overall teaching of Scripture on a subject. A confession gives us a tool for evaluating his understanding and teaching in summary form.

Though we may agree that confessions in general are useful, why would we use this particular confession? Why not a freshly written statement instead of a dusty old confession that is over 300 years old? First, the age of a confession should commend it rather than condemn it. Truth does not change. If the confession was accurate when it was composed, then it is accurate now. Those who hammered out the confession were men of a different day—men who had been refined by the fires of persecution. These were no arm-chair doctrines to them but a living faith that had stood up under trial. The men who first owned this confession were not those who were likely to bow to the spirit of the age—not their age and certainly not ours—either in their doctrine or their lives.

We now have the advantage of over 300 years to have examined the doctrines of the *1689 Confession* and to see its outworkings in the lives of churches and individuals. This confession more than any other in Baptist life has stood the test of time. The *1689 Confession* is the most mature statement of theology that has found broad acceptance among Particular (Calvinistic) Baptists. It is based broadly on the Presbyterian *Westminster Confession of Faith* (WCF). The WCF was hammered out by 121 divines who labored daily for two years (1644–1646) to express the doctrines of Scripture as understood in the light of the Reformation. The Independents followed in 1658 with the *Savoy Declaration*, a revision of the WCF that reflected their independent form of church government along with a few other changes and additions. The Baptists, finding the Savoy to be closer to their views of church government, modified this confession in the area of baptism and made further refinements. Their confession was composed and published by the Particular Baptist churches of England in 1677. It was subsequently adopted by a national assembly of Particular Baptists in 1689, giving it the nickname that is often used today. Thus, this confession had the privilege of standing on the shoulders of the giants of the Reformation and Puritan eras and the advantage of 31 intervening years for its authors to study and refine the statements of the WCF. This confession was able to express the common faith Particular Baptists shared with others having a Reformed heritage and also articulate their distinctive doctrines.

The *1689 Confession* has been in continuous usage since it was written. It was used widely not only in England but in America, beginning with the Philadelphia Association. The same confession was used in the South, and with one additional paragraph it became known as the Charleston Confession. The *1689 Confession* was the confessional statement of the church or association of every one of the 293 delegates who gathered in Augusta, Georgia, to organize the Southern Baptist Convention in 1845. It was also the doctrinal statement that Charles H. Spurgeon used in his church. At one time, it was so widely used that it was referred to simply as *The Baptist Confession*. The *Abstract of Principles* of two SBC seminaries is self-conscientiously an abstract or summary of this confession.

Such a time-tested statement of biblical doctrine can give us clarity beyond our present level of study. Here is how it works. As we study the various doctrines articulated by the confession, we find that the confession faithfully summarizes the teaching of Scripture in these areas. Then we realize that countless godly pastors, theologians, and churches sharing these same convictions through the centuries have held that they are part and parcel of a biblical system of doctrine that is summarized by the confession. Through this process we become increasingly confident that the parts we do not yet understand are just as biblical and mesh well with the parts that we do understand! This is a wonderful blessing to impart to new believers and those who are still investigating some aspects of our doctrine. There is safety and wisdom in beginning with a theological foundation reflecting the tried and proven faith of a large body of God's people rather than the relatively untested opinions of private individuals.

I have long wanted to update the language of the *1689 Confession* to make its blessings more accessible to modern readers. I am thankful for other modern versions, but I have also wanted to produce a version that is at the same time affordable, consistent and modern in style, and meticulously careful in preserving the meaning of the original. I have approached this effort with fear and trembling. Above all, I have wanted to preserve the doctrine and maintain the clarity of the original. I have circulated this effort widely and received helpful suggestions and corrections from many people, for which I am grateful. This has not been a solo effort.

My goal has been to maintain the structure and language to the extent that these lend themselves to clarity for the modern reader. When the structure or language was archaic, only then did I consider modern equivalent terms or rephrasing. In more difficult cases, I reworked the structure of a paragraph when it could be stated in a significantly more natural way in modern English without compromising the meaning. I don't pretend that the result is readable on a sixth-grade level. The concepts in the confession simply don't lend themselves to such simplistic expression. Furthermore, I have avoided changing well-established theological terms unless I judged that they were obscure and could be greatly clarified by a modern expression. In a few cases the meaning of the original term was unclear, or the term could not easily be rendered by an equivalent modern term. In these cases, I used footnotes. Footnotes in italics indicate the original term. Non-italic footnotes clarify the meaning.

I commend this modern-language version in the words of the preface to the original:

> We shall conclude with our earnest prayer, that the God of all grace, will pour out those measures of His holy Spirit upon us, that the profession of truth may be accompanied with the sound belief, and diligent practice of it by us; that His name may in all things be glorified, through Jesus Christ our Lord, Amen.

Stan Reeves
Auburn, Alabama

THE HOLY SCRIPTURES

1:1   The Holy Scriptures are the only sufficient, certain, and infallible standard of all saving knowledge, faith, and obedience.[1] The light of nature and the works of creation and providence so clearly demonstrate the goodness, wisdom, and power of God that people are left without excuse; however, these demonstrations are not sufficient to give the knowledge of God and His will that is necessary for salvation.[2] Therefore, the Lord was pleased at different times and in various ways to reveal Himself and to declare His will to His church.[3] To preserve and propagate the truth better and to establish and comfort the church with greater certainty against the corruption of the flesh and the malice of Satan and the world, the Lord put this revelation completely in writing. Therefore, the Holy Scriptures are absolutely necessary, because God's former ways of revealing His will to His people have now ceased.[4]

[1] 2 Timothy 3:15–17; Isaiah 8:20; Luke 16:29, 31; Ephesians 2:20. [2] Romans 1:19–21; Romans 2:14,15; Psalm 19:1–3. [3] Hebrews 1:1. [4] Proverbs 22:19–21; Romans 15:4; 2 Peter 1:19, 20.

1:2   The Holy Scriptures, or the Word of God written, consist of all the books of the Old and New Testaments. These are:

THE OLD TESTAMENT: Genesis, Exodus, Leviticus, Numbers, Deuteronomy, Joshua, Judges, Ruth, 1 Samuel, 2 Samuel, 1 Kings, 2 Kings, 1 Chronicles, 2 Chronicles, Ezra, Nehemiah, Esther, Job, Psalms, Proverbs, Ecclesiastes, Song of Solomon, Isaiah, Jeremiah, Lamentations, Ezekiel, Daniel, Hosea, Joel, Amos, Obadiah, Jonah, Micah, Nahum, Habakkuk, Zephaniah, Haggai, Zechariah, Malachi.

THE NEW TESTAMENT: Matthew, Mark, Luke, John, Acts, Romans, 1 Corinthians, 2 Corinthians, Galatians, Ephesians, Philippians, Colossians, 1 Thessalonians, 2 Thessalonians, 1 Timothy, 2 Timothy, Titus, Philemon, Hebrews, James, 1 Peter, 2 Peter, 1 John, 2 John, 3 John, Jude, Revelation.

All of these are given by the inspiration of God to be the standard of faith and life.[5]

[5]2 Timothy 3:16.

1:3 The books commonly called the Apocrypha were not given by divine inspiration and so are not part of the canon or standard of the Scriptures. Therefore, they have no authority for the church of God and are not to be recognized or used in any way different from other human writings.[6]

[6]Luke 24:27, 44; Romans 3:2.

1:4 The authority of the Holy Scriptures obligates belief in them. This authority does not depend on the testimony of any person or church but on God the author alone, who is truth itself. Therefore, the Scriptures are to be received because they are the Word of God.[7]

[7]2 Peter 1:19–21; 2 Timothy 3:16; 1 Thessalonians 2:13; 1 John 5:9.

1:5 The testimony of the church of God may stir and persuade us to adopt a high and reverent respect for the Holy Scriptures. Moreover, the heavenliness of the contents, the power of the system of truth, the majesty of the style, the harmony of all the parts, the central focus on giving all glory to God, the full revelation of the only way of salvation, and many other incomparable qualities and complete perfections, all provide abundant evidence that the Scriptures are the Word of God. Even so, our full persuasion and assurance of the infallible truth and divine authority of the Scriptures comes from the internal work of the Holy Spirit bearing witness by and with the Word in our hearts.[8]

[8]John 16:13,14; 1 Corinthians 2:10–12; 1 John 2:20, 27.

1:6 The whole counsel of God concerning everything essential for His own glory and man's salvation, faith, and life is either explicitly stated or by necessary inference contained in the Holy Scriptures. Nothing is ever to be added to the Scriptures, either by new revelation of the Spirit or by human traditions.[9]

Nevertheless, we acknowledge that the inward illumination of the Spirit of God is necessary for a saving understanding of what is revealed in the Word.[10] We recognize that some circumstances concerning the worship of God and government of the church are common to human actions and organizations and are to be ordered by the light of nature and Christian wisdom, following the general rules of the Word, which must always be observed.[11]

[9]2 Timothy 3:15–17; Galatians 1:8,9. [10]John 6:45; 1 Corinthians 2:9–12. [11]1 Corinthians 11:13, 14; 1 Corinthians 14:26, 40.

1:7   Some things in Scripture are clearer than others, and some people understand the teachings more clearly than others.[12] However, the things that must be known, believed, and obeyed for salvation are so clearly set forth and explained in one part of Scripture or another that both the educated and uneducated may achieve a sufficient understanding of them by properly using ordinary measures.[13]

[12]2 Peter 3:16. [13]Psalm 19:7; Psalm 119:130.

1:8   The Old Testament was written in Hebrew, the native language of the ancient people of God.[14] The New Testament was written in Greek, which at the time it was written was most widely known to the nations. These Testaments were inspired directly by God and by His unique care and providence were kept pure down through the ages. They are therefore true and authoritative,[a] so that in all religious controversies the church must make their ultimate appeal to them.[15] All God's people have a right to and a claim on the Scriptures and are commanded in the fear of God to read[16] and search them.[17] Not all of God's people know these original languages, so the Scriptures are to be translated into the common language of every nation to which they come.[18] In this way the Word of God may dwell richly in all, so that they may worship Him in an acceptable manner and through patience and the comfort of the Scriptures may have hope.[19]

[a]authentical. [14]Romans 3:2. [15]Isaiah 8:20. [16]Acts 15:15. [17]John 5:39. [18]1 Corinthians 14:6, 9, 11, 12, 24, 28. [19]Colossians 3:16.

1:9   The infallible rule for interpreting Scripture is the Scripture
      itself. Therefore, when there is a question about the true and
      full meaning[b] of any part of Scripture (and each passage has
      only one meaning, not many), it must be understood in light
      of other passages that speak more clearly.[20]

[b]*sense.* [20]2 Peter 1:20, 21; Acts 15:15, 16.

1:10 The supreme judge for deciding all religious controversies and
      for evaluating all decrees of councils, opinions of ancient writ-
      ers, human teachings, and individual interpretations[c], and in
      whose judgment we are to rest, is nothing but the Holy Scrip-
      ture delivered by the Spirit. In this Scripture our faith finds its
      final word.[21]

[c]*private spirits.* [21]Matthew 22:29, 31, 32; Ephesians 2:20; Acts 28:23.

II
GOD AND THE HOLY TRINITY

2:1   The Lord our God is one, the only living and true God.[1] He is
      self-existent[2] and infinite in being and perfection. His essence
      cannot be understood by anyone but Him.[3] He is a perfectly
      pure spirit.[4] He is invisible and has no body, parts, or change-
      able emotions.[a] He alone has immortality, dwelling in light that
      no one can approach.[5] He is unchangeable,[6] immense,[b,7] eter-
      nal,[8] incomprehensible, almighty,[9] in every way infinite, abso-
      lutely holy,[10] perfectly wise, wholly free, completely absolute.
      He works all things according to the counsel of His own un-
      changeable and completely righteous will[11] for His own glory.[12]
      He is most loving, gracious, merciful, and patient. He overflows
      with goodness and truth, forgiving iniquity, transgression, and
      sin. He rewards those who seek Him diligently.[13] At the same
      time, He is perfectly just and terrifying in His judgments.[14] He
      hates all sin[15] and will certainly not clear the guilty.[16]

[a]*passions.* [b]transcends all space. [1]1 Corinthians 8:4, 6; Deuteronomy
6:4. [2]Jeremiah 10:10; Isaiah 48:12. [3]Exodus 3:14. [4]John 4:24. [5]1 Timothy
1:17; Deuteronomy 4:15, 16. [6]Malachi 3:6. [7]1 Kings 8:27; Jeremiah

23:23. [8]Psalm 90:2. [9]Genesis 17:1. [10]Isaiah 6:3. [11]Psalm 115:3; Isaiah
46:10. [12]Proverbs 16:4; Romans 11:36. [13]Exodus 34:6, 7; Hebrews 11:6.
[14]Nehemiah 9:32, 33. [15]Psalm 5:5, 6. [16]Exodus 34:7; Nahum 1:2, 3.

2:2   God has all life,[17] glory,[18] goodness,[19] and blessedness in and
      of Himself; He alone is all-sufficient in Himself. He does not
      need any creature He has made nor does He derive any glory
      from them.[20] Instead, He demonstrates His own glory in them,
      by them, to them and upon them. He alone is the source of all
      being, and everything is from Him, through Him and to Him.[21]
      He has absolute sovereign rule over all creatures, to act through
      them, for them, or upon them as He pleases.[22] In His sight ev-
      erything is open and visible.[23] His knowledge is infinite and
      infallible. It does not depend upon any creature, so for Him
      nothing is contingent or uncertain.[24] He is absolutely holy in
      all His plans, in all His works,[25] and in all His commands. An-
      gels and human beings owe to Him all the worship,[26] service, or
      obedience that creatures owe to the Creator and whatever else
      He is pleased to require of them.

[17]John 5:26. [18]Psalm 148:13. [19]Psalm 119:68. [20]Job 22:2, 3. [21]Romans
11:34–36. [22]Daniel 4:25, 34, 35. [23]Hebrews 4:13. [24]Ezekiel 11:5; Acts 15:18.
[25]Psalm 145:17. [26]Revelation 5:12–14.

2:3   This divine and infinite Being consists of three real persons,[c]
      the Father, the Word or Son, and the Holy Spirit.[27] These three
      have the same substance, power, and eternity, each having the
      whole divine essence without this essence being divided.[28] The
      Father is not derived from anyone, neither begotten nor pro-
      ceeding. The Son is eternally begotten of the Father.[29] The Holy
      Spirit proceeds from the Father and the Son.[30] All three are in-
      finite and without beginning and are therefore only one God,
      who is not to be divided in nature and being. Yet these three
      are distinguished by several distinctive characteristics and per-
      sonal relations. This truth of the Trinity is the foundation of all
      of our fellowship with God and of our comforting dependence
      on Him.

[c]*subsistences,* or individual instances of a given essence. [27]1 John 5:7;
Matthew 28:19; 2 Corinthians 13:14. [28]Exodus 3:14; John 14:11;
1 Corinthians 8:6. [29]John 1:14,18. [30]John 15:26; Galatians 4:6.

III
GOD'S DECREE

3:1   From all eternity God decreed everything that occurs, with-
      out reference to anything outside Himself.[1] He did this by the
      perfectly wise and holy counsel of His own will, freely and un-
      changeably. Yet God did this in such a way that He is neither
      the author of sin nor has fellowship with any in their sin.[2] This
      decree does not violate the will of the creature or take away the
      free working or contingency of second causes. On the contrary,
      these are established by God's decree.[3] In this decree God's
      wisdom is displayed in directing all things, and His power and
      faithfulness are demonstrated in accomplishing His decree.[4]

[1]Isaiah 46:10; Ephesians 1:11; Hebrews 6:17; Romans 9:15, 18. [2]James 1:13;
1 John 1:5. [3]Acts 4:27, 28; John 19:11. [4]Numbers 23:19; Ephesians 1:3–5.

3:2   God knows everything that could happen under any given con-
      ditions.[5] However, His decree of anything is not based on fore-
      seeing it in the future or foreseeing that it would occur under
      such conditions.[6]

[5]Acts 15:18. [6]Romans 9:11, 13, 16, 18.

3:3   By God's decree, and for the demonstration of His glory, some
      human beings and angels are predestined (or foreordained) to
      eternal life through Jesus Christ,[7] to the praise of His glorious
      grace.[8] Others are left to live in their sin, leading to their just
      condemnation, to the praise of His glorious justice.[9]

[7]1 Timothy 5:21; Matthew 25:34. [8]Ephesians 1:5, 6. [9]Romans 9:22, 23;
Jude 4.

3:4   These predestined and foreordained angels and people are in-
      dividually and unchangeably designated, and their number is
      so certain and definite that it cannot be either increased or de-
      creased.[10]

[10]2 Timothy 2:19; John 13:18.

3:5 Those people who are predestined to life were chosen by God before the foundation of the world, according to His eternal and unchangeable purpose and the secret counsel and good pleasure of His will. He chose them in Christ for eternal glory, purely as a result of His free grace and love,[11] without anything else about them serving as a condition or cause moving Him to do so.[12]

[11]Ephesians 1:4, 9, 11; Romans 8:30; 2 Timothy 1:9; 1 Thessalonians 5:9.
[12]Romans 9:13, 16; Ephesians 2:5, 12.

3:6 Just as God has appointed the elect to glory, so He has by the eternal and completely free purpose of His will foreordained all the means.[13] Therefore, those who are elected, being fallen in Adam, are redeemed by Christ[14] and effectually called to faith in Christ by His Spirit working at the appropriate time. They are justified, adopted, sanctified,[15] and kept by His power through faith to salvation.[16] None but the elect are redeemed by Christ, or effectually called, justified, adopted, sanctified, and saved.[17]

[13]1 Peter 1:2; 2 Thessalonians 2:13. [14]1 Thessalonians 5:9, 10. [15]Romans 8:30; 2 Thessalonians 2:13. [16]1 Peter 1:5. [17]John 10:26; 17:9; 6:64.

3:7 The doctrine of the high mystery of predestination is to be handled with special prudence and care so that those heeding the will of God revealed in His Word and obeying Him may be assured of their eternal election by the certainty of their effectual calling.[18] In this way this doctrine will give reasons for praise,[19] reverence, and admiration of God, as well as humility,[20] diligence and rich comfort to all who sincerely obey the gospel.[21]

[18]1 Thessalonians 1:4, 5; 2 Peter 1:10. [19]Ephesians 1:6; Romans 11:33. [20]Romans 11:5, 6, 20. [21]Luke 10:20.

IV
CREATION

4:1   In the beginning God the Father, Son, and Holy Spirit[1] was
      pleased to create or make the world and all things in it, both
      visible and invisible, in a six-day period, and all very good.[2] He
      did this to manifest the glory of His eternal power, wisdom and
      goodness.[3]

[1]John 1:2, 3; Hebrews 1:2; Job 26:13. [2]Colossians 1:16; Genesis 1:31.
[3]Romans 1:20.

4:2   After God had made all the other creatures, He created human-
      ity. He made them male and female,[4] with rational and immor-
      tal souls,[5] thereby making them suited to that life lived unto
      God for which they were created. They were made in the image
      of God, being endowed with knowledge, righteousness, and
      true holiness.[6] They had the law of God written in their hearts[7]
      and the power to fulfill it. Even so, they could still transgress
      the law, because they were left to the liberty of their own will,
      which was subject to change.[8]

[4]Genesis 1:27. [5]Genesis 2:7. [6]Ecclesiastes 7:29; Genesis 1:26. [7]Romans
2:14, 15. [8]Genesis 3:6.

4:3   In addition to the law written in their hearts, they received a
      command not to eat from the tree of the knowledge of good
      and evil.[9] As long as they obeyed this command, they were
      happy in their communion with God and had dominion over
      the creatures.[10]

[9]Genesis 2:17; [10]Genesis 1:26, 28.

V
DIVINE PROVIDENCE

5:1 God the good Creator of all things, in His infinite power and wisdom, upholds, directs, arranges and governs all creatures and things,[1] from the greatest to the least,[2] by His perfectly wise and holy providence, to the purpose for which they were created. He governs according to His infallible foreknowledge and the free and unchangeable counsel of His own will. His providence leads to the praise of the glory of His wisdom, power, justice, infinite goodness and mercy.[3]

[1]Hebrews 1:3; Job 38:11; Isaiah 46:10, 11; Psalm 135:6. [2]Matthew 10:29-31. [3]Ephesians 1:11.

5:2 All things come to pass unchangeably and certainly in relation to the foreknowledge and decree of God,[4] who is the first cause. Thus, nothing happens to anyone by chance or outside of God's providence.[5] Yet by the same providence God arranges all things to occur according to the nature of second causes, either necessarily, freely, or in response to other causes.[6]

[4]Acts 2:23. [5]Proverbs 16:33. [6]Genesis 8:22.

5:3 In His ordinary providence, God makes use of means,[7] though He is free to work apart from them,[8] beyond them[9] and contrary to them[10] at His pleasure.

[7]Acts 27:31, 44; Isaiah 55:10, 11. [8]Hosea 1:7. [9]Romans 4:19-21. [10]Daniel 3:27.

5:4 The almighty power, unsearchable wisdom, and infinite goodness of God are so thoroughly demonstrated in His providence, that His sovereign plan includes even the first fall and every other sinful action both of angels and humans.[11] God's providence over sinful actions does not occur by simple permission but by a form of permission that God most wisely and powerfully limits and in other ways arranges and governs.[12] Through a complex arrangement of methods He channels sinful actions to accomplish His perfectly holy purposes.[13] Yet He does this in such a way that the sinfulness of their acts arises only from the creatures and not from God. Because God is altogether holy and righteous, He can neither originate nor approve of sin.[14]

[11]Romans 11:32–34; 2 Samuel 24:1, 1 Chronicles 21:1. [12]2 Kings 19:28; Psalm 76:10. [13]Genesis 50:20; Isaiah 10:6, 7, 12. [14]Psalm 50:21; 1 John 2:16.

5:5   The perfectly wise, righteous, and gracious God often allows His own children for a time to experience a variety of temptations and the sinfulness of their own hearts. He does this to chastise them for their former sins or to make them aware of the hidden strength of the corruption and deceitfulness of their hearts so that they may be humbled. He also does this to lead them to a closer and more constant dependence on Him to sustain them, to make them more cautious about all future circumstances that may lead to sin, and for other just and holy purposes.[15] So whatever happens to any of His elect happens by His appointment, for His glory and for their good.[16]

[15]2 Chronicles 32:25, 26, 31; 2 Corinthians 12:7–9. [16]Romans 8:28.

5:6   God, as the righteous Judge, sometimes blinds and hardens wicked and ungodly people because of their sins.[17] He withholds His grace from them, by which they could have been enlightened in their understanding and had their hearts renewed.[18] Not only that, but sometimes He also takes away the gifts they already had[19] and exposes them to situations that their corrupt natures turn into opportunities for sin.[20] Moreover, He gives them over to their own lusts, the temptations of the world, and the power of Satan,[21] so that they harden themselves in response to the same influences that God uses to soften others.[22]

[17]Romans 1:24–26, 28; Romans 11:7, 8. [18]Deuteronomy 29:4. [19]Matthew 13:12. [20]Deuteronomy 2:30; 2 Kings 8:12, 13. [21]Psalm 81:11, 12; 2 Thessalonians 2:10–12. [22]Exodus 8:15, 32; Isaiah 6:9, 10; 1 Peter 2:7, 8.

5:7   The providence of God in a general way includes all creatures, but in a special way it takes care of His church and arranges all things to its good.[23]

[23]1 Timothy 4:10; Amos 9:8, 9; Isaiah 43:3–5.

VI

THE FALL OF MANKIND, AND SIN AND ITS PUNISHMENT

6:1 God created humanity upright and perfect. He gave them a righteous law that would have led to life if they had kept it but threatened death if they broke it.[1] Yet they did not remain for long in this position of honor. Satan used the craftiness of the serpent to seduce Eve, who then seduced Adam. Adam acted without any outside compulsion and deliberately transgressed the law of their creation and the command given to them by eating the forbidden fruit.[2] God was pleased, in keeping with His wise and holy counsel, to permit this act, because He had purposed to direct it for His own glory.

[1]Genesis 2:16, 17. [2]Genesis 3:12, 13; 2 Corinthians 11:3.

6:2 By this sin our first parents fell from their original righteousness and communion with God. We fell in them, and through this, death came upon all.[3] All became dead in sin[4] and completely defiled in all the capabilities and parts of soul and body.[5]

[3]Romans 3:23. [4]Romans 5:12ff. [5]Titus 1:15; Genesis 6:5; Jeremiah 17:9; Romans 3:10–19.

6:3 By God's appointment, they were the root and the representatives of the whole human race. Because of this, the guilt of their sin was accounted, and their corrupt nature passed on, to all their offspring who descended from them by ordinary procreation.[6] Their descendants are now conceived in sin[7] and are by nature children of wrath,[8] the servants of sin, and partakers of death[9] and all other miseries—spiritual, temporal, and eternal—unless the Lord Jesus sets them free.[10]

[6]Romans 5:12–19; 1 Corinthians 15:21, 22, 45, 49. [7]Psalm 51:5; Job 14:4. [8]Ephesians 2:3. [9]Romans 6:20; 5:12. [10]Hebrews 2:14, 15; 1 Thessalonians 1:10.

6:4 All actual transgressions arise from this first corruption.[11] By it we are thoroughly biased against, and disabled and antagonistic toward all that is good, and we are completely inclined toward all that is evil.[12]

[11]James 1:14, 15; Matthew 15:19. [12]Romans 8:7; Colossians 1:21.

6:5 During this life, this corruption of nature remains in those who are regenerated.[13] Even though it is pardoned and put to death through Christ, yet both this corruption of nature and all actions arising from it are truly and actually sin.[14]

[13]Romans 7:18,23; Ecclesiastes 7:20; 1 John 1:8. [14]Romans 7:23–25; Galatians 5:17.

VII

GOD'S COVENANT

7:1 Though rational creatures are responsible to obey God as their Creator, the distance between God and these creatures is so great that they could never have attained the reward of life except by God's voluntary condescension. He has been pleased to express this through a covenant framework.[1]

[1]Luke 17:10; Job 35:7, 8.

7:2 Since humanity brought itself under the curse of the law by its fall, it pleased the Lord to make a covenant of grace.[2] In this covenant He freely offers to sinners life and salvation through Jesus Christ. On their part He requires faith in Him, that they may be saved,[3] and promises to give His Holy Spirit to all who are ordained to eternal life, to make them willing and able to believe.[4]

[2]Genesis 2:17; Galatians 3:10; Romans 3:20, 21. [3]Romans 8:3; Mark 16:15, 16; John 3:16. [4]Ezekiel 36:26, 27; John 6:44, 45; Psalm 110:3.

7:3 This covenant is revealed in the gospel. It was revealed first
of all to Adam in the promise of salvation through the seed
of the woman.[5] After that, it was revealed step by step until
the full revelation of it was completed in the New Testament.[6]
This covenant is based on the eternal covenant transaction between the Father and the Son concerning the redemption of
the elect.[7] Only through the grace of this covenant have those
saved from among the descendants of fallen Adam obtained
life and blessed immortality. Humanity is now utterly incapable of being accepted by God on the same terms on which
Adam was accepted in his state of innocence.[8]

[5]Genesis 3:15. [6]Hebrews 1:1. [7]2 Timothy 1:9; Titus 1:2; [8]Hebrews 11:6, 13;
Romans 4:1, 2ff.; Acts 4:12; John 8:56.

VII
CHRIST THE MEDIATOR

8:1 God was pleased, in His eternal purpose, to choose and ordain
the Lord Jesus, His only begotten Son, according to the covenant made between them, to be the mediator between God
and humanity.[1] God chose Him to be prophet,[2] priest[3] and
king,[4] and to be head and savior of the church,[5] the heir of all
things,[6] and judge of the world.[7] From all eternity, God gave
to the Son a people to be His offspring. In time these people
would be redeemed, called, justified, sanctified and glorified
by Him.[8]

[1]Isaiah 42:1; 1 Peter 1:19, 20. [2]Acts 3:22. [3]Hebrews 5:5, 6. [4]Psalm 2:6;
Luke 1:33. [5]Ephesians 1:22, 23. [6]Hebrews 1:2. [7]Acts 17:31. [8]Isaiah 53:10;
John 17:6; Romans 8:30.

8:2 The Son of God, the second person of the Holy Trinity, is truly
and eternally God. He is the brightness of the Father's glory,
the same in substance and equal with Him. He made the world
and sustains and governs everything He has made. When the

fullness of time came, He took upon Himself human nature, with all the essential properties and common weaknesses of it[9] but without sin.[10] He was conceived by the Holy Spirit in the womb of the Virgin Mary. The Holy Spirit came down upon her, and the power of the Most High overshadowed her. Thus, He was born of a woman from the tribe of Judah, a descendant of Abraham and David in fulfillment of the Scriptures.[11] Two whole, perfect, and distinct natures were inseparably joined together in one person, without converting one into the other or mixing them together to produce a different or blended nature. This person is truly God and truly man, yet one Christ, the only mediator between God and humanity.[12]

[9]John 1:14; Galatians 4;4. [10]Romans 8:3; Hebrews 2:14, 16, 17; Hebrews 4:15. [11]Matthew 1:22, 23; Luke 1:27, 31, 35. [12]Romans 9:5; 1 Timothy 2:5.

8:3   The Lord Jesus, in His human nature united in this way to the divine in the person of the Son, was sanctified and anointed with the Holy Spirit beyond measure.[13] He had in Himself all the treasures of wisdom and knowledge.[14] The Father was pleased to make all fullness dwell in Him[15] so that—being holy, harmless, undefiled,[16] and full of grace and truth[17]—He was thoroughly qualified to carry out the office of mediator and guarantor.[18] He did not take this office upon Himself but was called to it by His Father,[19] who put all power and judgment in His hand and commanded Him to carry them out.[20]

[13]Psalm 45:7; Acts 10:38; John 3:34. [14]Colossians 2:3. [15]Colossians 1:19. [16]Hebrews 7:26. [17]John 1:14. [18]Hebrews 7:22. [19]Hebrews 5:5. [20]John 5:22, 27; Matthew 28:18; Acts 2:36.

8:4   The Lord Jesus most willingly undertook this office.[21] To discharge it, He was born under the law[22] and perfectly fulfilled it. He also experienced the punishment that we deserved and that we should have endured and suffered.[23] He was made sin and a curse for us.[24] He endured extremely heavy sorrows in His soul and extremely painful sufferings in His body.[25] He was crucified and died and remained in a state of death, yet His body did not decay.[26] On the third day He arose from the dead[27] with the same body in which He suffered.[28] In this body He also ascended into heaven,[29] where He sits at the right hand of His

Father, interceding.[30] He will return to judge men and angels at the end of the age.[31]

[21]Psalm 40:7, 8; Hebrews 10:5–10; John 10:18. [22]Galatians 4:4; Matthew 3:15. [23]Galatians 3:13; Isaiah 53:6; 1 Peter 3:18. [24]2 Corinthians 5:21. [25]Matthew 26:37, 38; Luke 22:44; Matthew 27:46. [26]Acts 13:37. [27]1 Corinthians 15:3, 4. [28]John 20:25, 27. [29]Mark 16:19; Acts 1:9–11. [30]Romans 8:34; Hebrews 9:24. [31]Acts 10:42; Romans 14:9, 10; Acts 1:11; 2 Peter 2:4.

8:5 The Lord Jesus has fully satisfied the justice of God, obtained reconciliation, and purchased an everlasting inheritance in the kingdom of heaven for all those given to Him by the Father.[32] He has accomplished these things by His perfect obedience and sacrifice of Himself, which He once for all offered up to God through the eternal Spirit.[33]

[32]John 17:2; Hebrews 9:15. [33]Hebrews 9:14; Hebrews 10:14; Romans 3:25, 26.

8:6 The price of redemption was not actually paid by Christ till after His incarnation. Yet the virtue, efficacy and benefit of it was imparted to the elect in every age since the beginning of the world, in and by those promises, types, and sacrifices that revealed Him and pointed to Him as the seed that would bruise the serpent's head[34] and the Lamb slain from the foundation of the world.[35] He is the same yesterday and today and forever.[36]

[34]1 Corinthians 4:10; Hebrews 4:2; 1 Peter 1:10, 11. [35]Revelation 13:8. [36]Hebrews 13:8.

8:7 In His work of mediation, Christ acts according to both natures, by each nature doing what is appropriate to itself. Even so, because of the unity of the person, that which is appropriate to one nature is sometimes in Scripture attributed to the person under the designation of the other nature.[37]

[37]John 3:13; Acts 20:28.

8:8 To all those for whom Christ has obtained eternal redemption, He certainly and effectually applies and imparts it. He intercedes for them,[38] unites them to Himself by His Spirit, and reveals to them in and by His Word the mystery of sal-

vation. He persuades them to believe and obey[39] and governs
their hearts by His Word and Spirit.[40] He overcomes all their
enemies by His almighty power and wisdom,[41] using methods
and ways that are perfectly consistent with His wonderful and
unsearchable governance. All these things are by free and absolute grace, apart from any condition for obtaining it that is
foreseen in them.[42]

[38]John 6:37; John 10:15, 16; John 17:9; Romans 5:10. [39]John 17:6;
Ephesians 1:9; 1 John 5:20. [40]Romans 8:9, 14. [41]Psalm 110:1; 1 Corinthians
15:25, 26. [42]John 3:8; Ephesians 1:8.

8:9   This office of mediator between God and humanity is appro-
      priate for Christ alone, who is the prophet, priest and king of
      the church of God. This office may not be transferred from
      Him to anyone else, either in whole or in part.[43]

[43]1 Timothy 2:5.

8:10 The number and character of these offices is essential. Because
      we are ignorant, we need His prophetic office.[44] Because we are
      alienated from God and imperfect in the best of our service, we
      need His priestly office to reconcile us and present us to God
      as acceptable.[45] Because we are hostile and utterly unable to
      return to God, and so that we can be rescued and made secure
      from our spiritual enemies, we need His kingly office to con-
      vince, subdue, draw, sustain, deliver and preserve us for His
      heavenly kingdom.[46]

[44]John 1:18. [45]Colossians 1:21; Galatians 5:17. [46]John 16:8; Psalm 110:3;
Luke 1:74, 75.

IX
FREE WILL

9:1   God has endowed human will with natural liberty and pow-
      er to act on choices so that it is neither forced nor inherently
      bound by nature to do good or evil.[1]

[1]Matthew 17:12; James 1:14; Deuteronomy 30:19.

9:2 Humanity in the state of innocence had freedom and power to will and to do what was good and well-pleasing to God.[2] Yet this condition was unstable, so that humanity could fall from it.[3]

[2]Ecclesiastes 7:29. [3]Genesis 3:6.

9:3 Humanity, by falling into a state of sin, has completely lost all ability to choose any spiritual good that accompanies salvation.[4] Thus, people in their natural[a] state are absolutely opposed to spiritual good and dead in sin,[5] so that they cannot convert themselves by their own strength or prepare themselves for conversion.[6]

[a]without the Spirit [4]Romans 5:6; Romans 8:7. [5]Ephesians 2:1, 5. [6]Titus 3:3–5; John 6:44.

9:4 When God converts sinners and transforms them into the state of grace, He frees them from their natural bondage to sin[7] and by His grace alone enables them to will and to do freely what is spiritually good.[8] Yet because of their remaining corruption, they do not perfectly nor exclusively will what is good but also will what is evil.[9]

[7]Colossians 1:13; John 8:36. [8]Philippians 2:13. [9]Romans 7:15, 18, 19, 21, 23.

9:5 Only in the state of glory is the will made perfectly and unchangeably free toward good alone.[10]

[10]Ephesians 4:13.

X
EFFECTUAL CALLING

10:1 In God's appointed and acceptable time, He is pleased to call effectually,[1] by His Word and Spirit, those He has predestined to life. He calls them out of their natural state of sin and death to grace and salvation by Jesus Christ.[2] He enlightens their minds spiritually and savingly to understand the things of God.[3] He takes away their heart of stone and gives them a heart of flesh.[4] He renews their wills and by His almighty power turns them to good and effectually draws them to Jesus Christ.[5] Yet He does all this in such a way that they come completely freely, since they are made willing by His grace.[6]

[1]Romans 8:30; Romans 11:7; Ephesians 1:10, 11; 2 Thessalonians 2:13, 14. [2]Ephesians 2:1–6. [3]Acts 26:18; Ephesians 1:17, 18. [4]Ezekiel 36:26. [5]Deuteronomy 30:6; Ezekiel 36:27; Ephesians 1:19. [6]Psalm 110:3; Song of Solomon 1:4.

10:2 This effectual call flows from God's free and special grace alone, not from anything at all foreseen in those called. Neither does the call arise from any power or action on their part;[7] they are totally passive in it. They are dead in sins and trespasses until they are made alive and renewed by the Holy Spirit.[8] By this they are enabled to answer this call and to embrace the grace offered and conveyed in it. This response is enabled by a power that is no less than that which raised Christ from the dead.[9]

[7]2 Timothy 1:9; Ephesians 2:8. [8]1 Corinthians 2:14; Ephesians 2:5; John 5:25. [9]Ephesians 1:19, 20.

10:3 Elect infants dying in infancy are regenerated and saved by Christ through the Spirit,[10] who works when and where and how He pleases.[11] The same is true of every elect person who is incapable of being outwardly called by the ministry of the Word.

[10]John 3:3, 5, 6. [11]John 3:8.

10:4 Those who are not elected will not and cannot truly come to Christ and therefore cannot be saved, because they are not effectually drawn by the Father.[12] They may even be called by the ministry of the Word and may receive some ordinary working of the Spirit without being saved.[13] Much less can any be saved who do not receive the Christian religion, no matter how diligently they live their lives according to the light of nature and the teachings of the religion they profess.[14]

[12]John 6:44, 45, 65; 1 John 2:24, 25. [13]Matthew 22:14; Matthew 13:20, 21; Hebrews 6:4, 5. [14]Acts 4:12; John 4:22; John 17:3.

XI
JUSTIFICATION

11:1   Those God effectually calls He also freely justifies.[1] He does this, not by infusing righteousness into them but by pardoning their sins and accounting and accepting them as righteous.[2] He does this for Christ's sake alone and not for anything produced in them or done by them.[3] He does not impute faith itself, the act of believing, or any other gospel obedience to them as their righteousness. Instead, He imputes Christ's active obedience to the whole law and passive obedience in His death as their whole and only righteousness by faith.[4] This faith is not self-generated; it is the gift of God.[5]

[1]Romans 3:24; 8:30. [2]Romans 4:5–8; Ephesians 1:7. [3]1 Corinthians 1:30, 31; Romans 5:17–19. [4]Philippians 3:8, 9; Ephesians 2:8–10. [5]John 1:12; Romans 5:17.

11:2   Faith that receives and rests on Christ and His righteousness is the only instrument of justification.[6] Yet it does not occur by itself in the person justified, but it is always accompanied by every other saving grace. It is not a dead faith but works through love.[7]

[6]Romans 3:28. [7]Galatians 5:6; James 2:17, 22, 26.

11:3   By His obedience and death, Christ fully paid the debt of all those who are justified. He endured in their place the penalty they deserved. By this sacrifice of Himself in His bloodshed on the cross, He legitimately, really and fully satisfied God's justice on their behalf.[8] Yet their justification is based entirely on free grace, because He was given by the Father for them, and His obedience and satisfaction were accepted in their place. These things were done freely, not because of anything in them,[9] so that both the exact justice and the rich grace of God would be glorified in the justification of sinners.[10]

[8]Hebrews 10:14; 1 Peter 1:18, 19; Isaiah 53:5, 6. [9]Romans 8:32; 2 Corinthians 5:21. [10]Romans 3:26; Ephesians 1:6,7; 2:7.

11:4 From all eternity God decreed to justify all the elect,[11] and in the fullness of time Christ died for their sins and rose again for their justification.[12] Nevertheless, they are not justified personally until the Holy Spirit actually applies Christ to them at the proper time.[13]

[11]Galatians 3:8; 1 Peter 1:2; 1 Timothy 2:6. [12]Romans 4:25. [13]Colossians 1:21, 22; Titus 3:4-7.

11:5 God continues to forgive the sins of those who are justified.[14] Even though they can never fall from a state of justification,[15] they may fall under God's fatherly displeasure because of their sins.[16] In that condition they will not usually have the light of His face restored to them until they humble themselves, confess their sins, plead for pardon, and renew their faith and repentance.[17]

[14]Matthew 6:12; 1 John 1:7, 9. [15]John 10:28. [16]Psalm 89:31-33. [17]Psalm 32:5; Psalm 51; Matthew 26:75.

11:6 In all these ways, the justification of believers under the Old Testament was exactly the same as the justification of believers under the New Testament.[18]

[18]Galatians 3:9; Romans 4:22-24.

XII
ADOPTION

12:1 God has granted that all those who are justified would receive the grace of adoption, in and for the sake of His only Son Jesus Christ.[1] By this they are counted among the children of God and enjoy the freedom and privileges of that relationship.[2] They inherit His name,[3] receive the spirit of adoption,[4] have access to the throne of grace with boldness, and are enabled to cry "Abba, Father!"[5] They are given compassion,[6] protected,[7] provided for[8] and chastened by Him as a father.[9] Yet they are never cast off[10] but are sealed for the day of redemption[11] and inherit the promises as heirs of everlasting salvation.[12]

[1]Ephesians 1:5; Galatians 4:4, 5. [2]John 1:12; Romans 8:17. [3]2 Corinthians 6:18; Revelation 3:12. [4]Romans 8:15. [5]Galatians 4:6; Ephesians 2:18. [6]Psalm 103:13. [7]Proverbs 14:26. [8]1 Peter 5:7. [9]Hebrews 12:6. [10]Isaiah 54:8, 9; Lamentations 3:31. [11]Ephesians 4:30. [12]Hebrews 1:14; 6:12.

XIII
SANCTIFICATION

13:1 Those who are united to Christ and effectually called and re-generated have a new heart and a new spirit created in them through the power of Christ's death and resurrection. They are also further sanctified, really and personally,[1] through the same power, by His Word and Spirit dwelling in them.[2] The do-minion of the whole body of sin is destroyed,[3] and the various evil desires that arise from it are more and more weakened and put to death.[4] At the same time, those called and regenerated are more and more enlivened and strengthened in all saving graces[5] so that they practice true holiness, without which no one will see the Lord.[6]

[1]Acts 20:32; Romans 6:5, 6. [2]John 17:17; Ephesians 3:16–19; 1 Thessalonians 5:21–23. [3]Romans 6:14. [4]Galatians 5:24. [5]Colossians 1:11. [6]2 Corinthians 7:1; Hebrews 12:14.

13:2 This sanctification extends throughout the whole person,[7] though it is never completed in this life. Some corruption re-mains in every part.[8] From this arises a continual and irreconcilable war, with the desires of the flesh against the Spirit and the Spirit against the flesh.[9]

[7]1 Thessalonians 5:23. [8]Romans 7:18, 23. [9]Galatians 5:17; 1 Peter 2:11.

13:3 In this war, the remaining corruption may greatly prevail for a time.[10] Yet through the continual supply of strength from the sanctifying Spirit of Christ, the regenerate part overcomes.[11]

So the saints grow in grace, perfecting holiness in the fear of God. They pursue a heavenly life, in gospel obedience to all the commands that Christ as Head and King has given them in His Word.[12]

[10]Romans 7:23. [11]Romans 6:14. [12]Ephesians 4:15, 16; 2 Corinthians 3:18; 2 Corinthians 7:1.

XIV
SAVING FAITH

14:1 The grace of faith enables the elect to believe so that their souls are saved; it is the work of the Spirit of Christ in their hearts.[1] Faith is ordinarily produced by the ministry of the Word.[2] By this same ministry and by the administration of baptism and the Lord's supper, prayer, and other means appointed by God, faith is increased and strengthened.[3]

[1]2 Corinthians 4:13; Ephesians 2:8. [2]Romans 10:14, 17. [3]Luke 17:5; 1 Peter 2:2; Acts 20:32.

14:2 By this faith Christians believe to be true everything revealed in the Word, recognizing it as the authority of God Himself.[4] They also perceive that the Word is more excellent than every other writing and everything else in the world,[5] because it displays the glory of God in His attributes, the excellence of Christ in His nature and offices, and the power and fullness of the Holy Spirit in His activities and operations. So they are enabled to entrust their souls to the truth believed.[6] They respond differently according to the content of each particular passage—obeying the commands,[7] trembling at the threatenings,[8] and embracing the promises of God for this life and the one to come.[9] But the principal acts of saving faith focus directly on Christ—accepting, receiving, and resting upon Him alone for justification, sanctification and eternal life, by virtue of the covenant of grace.[10]

[4]Acts 24:14. [5]Psalm 27:7–10; Psalm 119:72. [6]2 Timothy 1:12. [7]John 14:14.

[8]Isaiah 66:2. [9]Hebrews 11:13. [10]John 1:12; Acts 16:31; Galatians 2:20; Acts 15:11.

14:3 This faith may exist in varying degrees so that it may be either weak or strong.[11] Yet even in its weakest form, it is different in kind or nature (like all other saving graces) from the faith and common grace of temporary believers.[12] Therefore, faith may often be attacked and weakened, but it gains the victory.[13] It matures in many to the point that they attain full assurance through Christ,[14] who is both the founder and perfecter of our faith.[15]

[11]Hebrews 5:13, 14; Matthew 6:30; Romans 4:19, 20. [12]2 Peter 1:1. [13]Ephesians 6:16; 1 John 5:4, 5. [14]Hebrews 6:11, 12; Colossians 2:2. [15]Hebrews 12:2.

XV
REPENTANCE TO LIFE
AND SALVATION

15:1 Some of the elect are converted after their early years, having lived in the natural[a] state for a time and served various evil desires and pleasures. God gives these repentance to life as part of their effectual calling.[1]

[a]without the Spirit. [1]Titus 3:2–5.

15:2 There is no one who does good and does not sin.[2] Even the best may fall into great sins and offenses, through the power and deceitfulness of the corruption in them, along with the strength of temptation. Therefore, God has mercifully provided in the covenant of grace that believers who sin and fall will be renewed through repentance to salvation.[3]

[2]Ecclesiastes 7:20. [3]Luke 22:31, 32.

15:3 This saving repentance is a gospel grace[4] in which those who are made aware by the Holy Spirit of the many evils of their sin, by faith in Christ humble themselves for it with godly sorrow, hatred of it, and self-loathing.[5] They pray for pardon and strength of grace and determine and endeavor by provisions from the Spirit to live before God in a well-pleasing way in everything.[6]

[4]Zechariah 12:10; Acts 11:18. [5]Ezekiel 36:31; 2 Corinthians 7:11. [6]Psalm 119:6, 128.

15:4 Repentance must continue throughout our lives, because of the body of death and its activities. So it is everyone's duty to repent of each specific, known sin specifically.[7]

[7]Luke 19:8; 1 Timothy 1:13, 15.

15:5 God has made full provision through Christ in the covenant of grace to preserve believers in their salvation. Thus, although there is no sin so small that it is undeserving of damnation,[8] yet there is no sin so great that it will bring damnation on those who repent.[9] This makes the constant preaching of repentance necessary.

[8]Romans 6:23. [9]Isaiah 1:16–18; 55:7.

XVI
GOOD WORKS

16:1 Good works are only those works that God has commanded in His holy Word.[1] Works that do not have this warrant are invented by people out of blind zeal or on a pretense of good intentions and are not truly good.[2]

[1]Micah 6:8; Hebrews 13:21. [2]Matthew 15:9; Isaiah 29:13.

16:2 These good works, done in obedience to God's commandments, are the fruit and evidence of a true and living faith.[3] Through good works believers express their thankfulness,[4] strengthen their assurance,[5] build up their brothers and sisters, adorn the profession of the gospel,[6] stop the mouths of opponents, and glorify God.[7] Believers are God's workmanship, created in Christ Jesus for good works,[8] so that they bear fruit leading to holiness and have the outcome, eternal life.[9]

[3]James 2:18, 22. [4]Psalm 116:12, 13. [5]1 John 2:3, 5; 2 Peter 1:5–11. [6]Matthew 5:16. [7]1 Timothy 6:1; 1 Peter 2:15; Philippians 1:11. [8]Ephesians 2:10. [9]Romans 6:22.

16:3   Their ability to do good works does not arise at all from themselves but entirely from the Spirit of Christ.[10] To enable them to do good works, they need—in addition to the graces they have already received—an active influence of the same Holy Spirit to work in them to will and to do His good pleasure.[11] Yet this is no reason for them to grow negligent, as if they were not required to perform any duty without a special motion of the Spirit. Instead, they should be diligent to stir up the grace of God that is in them.[12]

[10]John 15:4, 5. [11]2 Corinthians 3:5; Philippians 2:13; [12]Philippians 2:12; Hebrews 6:11, 12; Isaiah 64:7.

16:4   Those who attain the greatest heights of obedience possible in this life are far from being able to merit reward by going beyond duty[a] or to do more than God requires. Instead, they fall short of much that is their duty to do.[13]

[a]supererogate. [13]Job 9:2, 3; Galatians 5:17; Luke 17:10.

16:5   We cannot, even by our best works, merit pardon of sin or eternal life from God's hand, due to the huge disproportion between our works and the glory to come, and the infinite distance between us and God. By these works we can neither benefit God nor satisfy Him for the debt of our former sins.[14] When we have done all we can, we have only done our duty and are unprofitable servants. Since our good works are good, they must proceed from His Spirit;[15] and since they are performed by us, they are defiled and mixed with so much weakness and imperfection that they cannot withstand the severity of God's punishment.[16]

[14]Romans 3:20; Ephesians 2:8, 9; Romans 4:6. [15]Galatians 5:22, 23. [16]Isaiah 64:6; Psalm 143:2.

16:6   Nevertheless, believers are accepted through Christ, and thus their good works are also accepted in Him.[17] This acceptance does not mean our good works are completely blameless and irreproachable in God's sight. Instead, God views them in His Son, and so He is pleased to accept and reward that which is sincere, even though it is accompanied by many weaknesses and imperfections.[18]

[17]Ephesians 1:6; 1 Peter 2:5. [18]Matthew 25:21, 23; Hebrews 6:10.

16:7   Works done by unregenerate people may in themselves be commanded by God and useful to themselves and others.[19] Yet they do not come from a heart purified by faith[20] and are not done in a right manner according to the Word[21] nor with a right goal—the glory of God.[22] Therefore, they are sinful and cannot please God. They cannot qualify anyone to receive grace from God,[23] and yet their neglect is even more sinful and displeasing to God.[24]

[19]2 Kings 10:30; 1 Kings 21:27, 29. [20]Genesis 4:5; Hebrews 11:4, 6. [21]1 Corinthians 13:1. [22]Matthew 6:2, 5. [23]Amos 5:21, 22; Romans 9:16; Titus 3:5. [24]Job 21:14, 15; Matthew 25:41-43.

XVII

PERSEVERANCE
OF THE SAINTS

17:1   Those God has accepted in the Beloved, effectually called and sanctified by His Spirit, and given the precious faith of His elect can neither totally nor finally fall from a state of grace. They will certainly persevere in grace to the end and be eternally saved, because the gifts and callings of God are irrevocable. Therefore, He still brings about and nourishes in them faith, repentance, love, joy, hope and all the graces of the Spirit that lead to immortality.[1] Even though many storms and floods arise and beat against them, yet these things will never be able to move the elect from the foundation and rock to which they are anchored by faith. The felt sight of the light and love of God may be clouded and obscured from them for a time through their unbelief and the temptations of Satan.[2] Yet God is still the same; they will certainly be kept by the power of God for salvation, where they will enjoy their purchased possession. For they are engraved on the palms of His hands, and their names have been written in the book of life from all eternity.[3]

[1]John 10:28, 29; Philippians 1:6; 2 Timothy 2:19; 1 John 2:19. [2]Psalm 89:31, 32; 1 Corinthians 11:32. [3]Malachi 3:6.

17:2 This perseverance of the saints does not depend on their own free will but on the unchangeableness of the decree of election,[4] which flows from the free and unchangeable love of God the Father. It is based on the efficacy of the merit and intercession of Jesus Christ and union with Him,[5] the oath of God,[6] the abiding of His Spirit, the seed of God within them,[7] and the nature of the covenant of grace.[8] The certainty and infallibility of their perseverance is based on all these things.

[4]Romans 8:30 Romans 9:11, 16. [5]Romans 5:9, 10; John 14:19. [6]Hebrews 6:17, 18. [7]1 John 3:9. [8]Jeremiah 32:40.

17:3 They may fall into grievous sins and continue in them for a time, due to the temptation of Satan and the world, the strength of corruption remaining in them, and the neglect of means of their preservation.[9] In so doing, they incur God's displeasure and grieve His Holy Spirit;[10] their graces and comforts become impaired;[11] their hearts are hardened and their consciences wounded;[12] they hurt and scandalize others and bring temporary judgments on themselves.[13] Nevertheless, they will renew their repentance and be preserved through faith in Christ Jesus to the end.[14]

[9]Matthew 26:70, 72, 74. [10]Isaiah 64:5, 9; Ephesians 4:30. [11]Psalm 51:10, 12. [12]Psalm 32:3, 4. [13]2 Samuel 12:14. [14]Luke 22:32, 61, 62.

XVIII

ASSURANCE OF GRACE
AND SALVATION

18:1 Temporary believers and other unregenerate people may de-
ceive themselves in vain with false hopes and fleshly presump-
tions that they have God's favor and salvation, but their hope
will perish.[1] Yet those who truly believe in the Lord Jesus and
love Him sincerely, endeavoring to walk in all good conscience
before Him, may be certainly assured in this life that they are
in a state of grace. They may rejoice in the hope of the glory of
God,[2] and this hope will never make them ashamed.[3]

[1]Job 8:13, 14; Matthew 7:22, 23. [2]1 John 2:3; 3:14, 18, 19, 21, 24; 5:13.
[3]Romans 5:2, 5.

18:2 This certainty is not merely an inconclusive or likely persuasion based on a fallible hope. It is an infallible assurance of
faith[4] founded on the blood and righteousness of Christ revealed in the gospel.[5] It is also built on the inward evidence
of those graces of the Spirit about which promises are made.[6]
It is further based on the testimony of the Spirit of adoption,
witnessing with our spirits that we are the children of God.[7] As
a fruit of this assurance, our hearts are kept both humble and
holy.[8]

[4]Hebrews 6:11, 19. [5]Hebrews 6:17, 18. [6]2 Peter 1:4, 5, 10, 11. [7]Romans 8:15,
16. [8]1 John 3:1–3.

18:3 This infallible assurance is not such an essential part of faith
that it is always fully experienced alongside faith,[a] but true believers may wait a long time and struggle with many difficulties before obtaining it.[9] Yet with the enabling of the Spirit to
know the things freely given to them by God, they may attain
this assurance using ordinary means appropriately without any
extraordinary revelation.[10] Therefore, it is the duty of all to be
as diligent as possible to make their calling and election sure.
In this way their hearts may be enlarged in peace and joy in the

Holy Spirit, in love and thankfulness to God, and in strength and cheerfulness in the duties of obedience. These effects are the natural fruits of this assurance.[11] Thus, it does not at all encourage believers to be negligent.[12]

[a]Phrase in italics added to clarify meaning. [9]Isaiah 50:10; Psalm 88; 77:1–12. [10]1 John 4:13; Hebrews 6:11, 12. [11]Romans 5:1, 2, 5; 14:17; Psalm 119:32. [12]Romans 6:1, 2; Titus 2:11, 12, 14.

18:4 True believers may in various ways have the assurance of their salvation shaken, decreased, or temporarily lost. This may happen because they neglect to preserve it[13] or fall into some specific sin that wounds their conscience and grieves the Spirit.[14] It may happen through some unexpected or forceful temptation[15] or when God withdraws the light of His face and allows even those who fear Him to walk in darkness and to have no light.[16] Yet they are never completely lacking the seed of God,[17] the life of faith,[18] love of Christ and the brethren, sincerity of heart, or conscience concerning their duty. Out of these graces, through the work of the Spirit, this assurance may at the proper time be revived.[19] In the meantime, they are kept from utter despair through them.[20]

[13]Song of Solomon 5:2, 3, 6. [14]Psalm 51:8, 12, 14. [15]Psalm 116:11; 77:7, 8; 31:22; [16]Psalm 30:7. [17]1 John 3:9. [18]Luke 22:32. [19]Psalm 42:5, 11. [20]Lamentations 3:26–31.

XIX
THE LAW OF GOD

19:1 God gave Adam a law of comprehensive obedience written in his heart and a specific precept not to eat the fruit of the tree of the knowledge of good and evil.[1] By these God obligated him and all his descendants to personal, total, exact and perpetual obedience.[2] God promised life if Adam fulfilled it and threatened death if he broke it, and He gave Adam the power and ability to keep it.[3]

[1]Genesis 1:27; Ecclesiastes 7:29. [2]Romans 10:5. [3]Galatians 3:10, 12.

19:2 The same law that was first written in the human heart continued to be a perfect rule of righteousness after the fall.[4] It was
delivered by God on Mount Sinai in ten commandments and
was written in two tables. The first four commandments con-
tain our duty to God and the other six our duty to humanity.[5]

[4]Romans 2:14, 15. [5]Deuteronomy 10:4.

19:3 In addition to this law—usually called the moral law—God was
pleased to give the people of Israel ceremonial laws, containing
several typological ordinances. In some ways these concerned
worship, by prefiguring Christ, His graces, actions, sufferings,
and benefits.[6] In other ways they revealed various instructions
about moral duties.[7] Since all of these ceremonial laws were
appointed only until the new order[a] arrived, they are now abol-
ished and taken away by Jesus Christ. As the true Messiah and
the only lawgiver, He was empowered by the Father to do this.[8]

[a]reformation. [6]Hebrews 10:1; Colossians 2:17. [7]1 Corinthians 5:7.
[8]Colossians 2:14, 16, 17; Ephesians 2:14, 16.

19:4 To Israel He also gave various judicial laws, which ceased at the
same time their nation ended. These laws no longer obligate
anyone as part of that institution. Only their general principles
of justice continue to have moral value.[9]

[9]1 Corinthians 9:8–10.

19:5 The moral law forever requires obedience of everyone, both
those who are justified as well as others.[10] This obligation arises
not only because of its content but also because of the authority of God the Creator who gave it.[11] Nor does Christ in any
way dissolve this obligation in the gospel; instead, He greatly
strengthens it.[12]

[10]Romans 13:8–10; James 2:8, 10–12. [11]James 2:10, 11. [12]Matthew 5:17–19;
Romans 3:31.

19:6 True believers are not under the law as a covenant of works, to
be justified or condemned by it.[13] Yet it is very useful to them
and to others as a rule of life that informs them of the will of
God and their duty. It directs and obligates them to live according to its precepts. It also exposes the sinful corruptions of

their natures, hearts, and lives. As they examine themselves in light of the law, they come to further conviction of, humiliation for, and hatred of sin,[14] along with a clearer view of their need for Christ and the perfection of His obedience. The law is also useful to the regenerate to restrain their corruptions because it forbids sin. The punishment threatened by the law shows them what even their sins deserve and what troubles they may expect in this life due to their sin, even though they are freed from the curse and undiminished severity of it. The promises of the law likewise show them God's approval of obedience and the blessings they may expect when they keep it, even though these blessings are not owed to them by the law as a covenant of works. If people do good and refrain from evil because the law encourages good and discourages evil, that does not indicate that they are under the law and not under grace.[15]

[13]Romans 6:14; Galatians 2:16; Romans 8:1; 10:4. [14]Romans 3:20; 7:7, etc; [15]Romans 6:12–14; 1 Peter 3:8–13.

19:7 These uses of the law are not contrary to the grace of the gospel but are in sweet harmony with it,[16] for the Spirit of Christ subdues and enables the human will to do freely and cheerfully what the will of God as revealed in the law requires.[17]

[16]Galatians 3:21. [17]Ezekiel 36:27.

XX
THE GOSPEL AND THE EXTENT
OF ITS GRACE

20:1 Because the covenant of works was broken by sin and was unable to confer life, God was pleased to proclaim the promise of Christ, the seed of the woman, as the means of calling the elect and producing in them faith and repentance.[1] In this promise the gospel in its substance was revealed and made effectual for the conversion and salvation of sinners.[2]

[1]Genesis 3:15. [2]Revelation 13:8.

20:2   This promise of Christ and of salvation through Him is re-
       vealed in the Word of God alone.[3] The works of creation and
       providence, when assisted only by the light of nature, do not
       reveal Christ or grace through Him, even in a general or ob-
       scure way.[4] Much less are those without the revelation of Him
       in the promise or gospel enabled to attain saving faith or re-
       pentance by seeing these works of God.[5]

   [3]Romans 1:17. [4]Romans 10:14, 15, 17. [5]Proverbs 29:18; Isaiah 25:7; Isaiah
   60:2, 3.

20:3   The gospel has been revealed to sinners in various times and
       in different places, along with the promises and precepts de-
       scribing the obedience it requires. The particular nations and
       individuals who are granted this revelation are chosen solely
       according to the sovereign will and good pleasure of God.[6]
       This choice does not depend on any promise to those who
       demonstrate good stewardship of their natural abilities based
       on common light received apart from the gospel. No one has
       ever done this nor can anyone do so.[7] Therefore, in every age
       the preaching of the gospel to individuals and nations has
       been granted in widely varying degrees of expansion and con-
       traction, according to the counsel of the will of God.

   [6]Psalm 147:20; Acts 16:7. [7]Romans 1:18–32.

20:4   The gospel is the only outward means of revealing Christ and
       saving grace, and it is abundantly sufficient for that purpose.
       Yet to be born again, brought to life or regenerated, those who
       are dead in trespasses also must have an effectual, irresistible
       work of the Holy Spirit in every part of their souls to produce
       in them a new spiritual life.[8] Without this no other means will
       bring about their conversion to God.[9]

   [8]Psalm 110:3; 1 Corinthians 2:14; Ephesians 1:19, 20. [9]John 6:44;
   2 Corinthians 4:4, 6.

XXI
CHRISTIAN LIBERTY AND
LIBERTY OF CONSCIENCE

21:1 The liberty Christ has purchased for believers under the gospel is found in their freedom from the guilt of sin, the condemning wrath of God, and the severity and curse of the law.[1] It also includes their deliverance from this present evil age,[2] bondage to Satan,[3] the dominion of sin,[4] the suffering of afflictions,[5] the fear and sting of death, the victory of the grave,[6] and everlasting damnation.[7] In addition, it includes their free access to God and their obedience to Him, not from slavish fear[8] but from a childlike love and willing mind.[9]

All these liberties were also enjoyed in their essence by believers under the law.[10] But under the New Testament the liberty of Christians is further expanded. They are free from the yoke of the ceremonial law to which the Jewish congregation was subjected; they have greater confidence of access to the throne of grace; and they have a fuller supply of God's free Spirit than believers under the law usually experienced.[11]

[1]Galatians 3:13. [2]Galatians 1:4. [3]Acts 26:18. [4]Romans 8:3. [5]Romans 8:28. [6]1 Corinthians 15:54–57. [7]2 Thessalonians 1:10. [8]Romans 8:15. [9]Luke 1:73–75; 1 John 4:18. [10]Galatians 3:9, 14. [11]John 7:38, 39; Hebrews 10:19–21.

21:2 God alone is Lord of the conscience,[12] and He has left it free from human doctrines and commandments that are in any way contrary to His Word or not contained in it.[13] So, believing such doctrines, or obeying such commands out of conscience, is a betrayal of true liberty of conscience.[14] Requiring implicit faith or absolute and blind obedience destroys liberty of conscience and reason as well.[15]

[12]James 4:12; Romans 14:4. [13]Acts 4:19, 29; 1 Corinthians 7:23; Matthew 15:9. [14]Colossians 2:20, 22, 23. [15]1 Corinthians 3:5; 2 Corinthians 1:24.

21:3 Those who use Christian liberty as an excuse to practice any sin or nurture any sinful desire pervert the main objective of the grace of the gospel to their own destruction,[16] and they completely destroy the purpose of Christian liberty. This purpose is that we, having been delivered from the hands of all our enemies, may serve the Lord without fear, in holiness and righteousness before Him, all the days of our lives.[17]

[16]Romans 6:1, 2. [17]Galatians 5:13; 2 Peter 2:18, 21.

XXII
Religious Worship and The Sabbath Day

22:1   The light of nature demonstrates that there is a God who has lordship and sovereignty over all. He is just and good and does good to everyone. Therefore, He should be feared, loved, praised, called on, trusted in and served—with all the heart and all the soul and all the strength.[1] But the acceptable way to worship the true God is instituted by Him,[2] and it is delimited by His own revealed will. Thus, He may not be worshipped according to human imagination or inventions or the suggestions of Satan, nor through any visible representations, nor in any other way that is not prescribed in the Holy Scriptures.[3]

[1]Jeremiah 10:7; Mark 12:33. [2]Deuteronomy 12:32. [3]Exodus 20:4–6.

22:2   Religious worship is to be given to God the Father, Son, and Holy Spirit and to Him alone[4]—not to angels, saints, or any other creatures.[5] Since the fall, worship is not to be given without a mediator[6] nor through any mediation other than of Christ alone.[7]

[4]Matthew 4:9, 10; John 5:23; Matthew 28:19. [5]Romans 1:25; Colossians 2:18; Revelation 19:10. [6]John 14:6. [7]1 Timothy 2:5.

22:3   Prayer with thanksgiving is an element of natural worship and so is required by God of everyone.[8] But to be acceptable, it must be made in the name of the Son,[9] by the help of the Spirit,[10] according to His will.[11] It must be accompanied by understanding, reverence, humility, fervor, faith, love and perseverance. Prayer with others must be in a language that is understood.[12]

[8]Psalm 95:1–7; 65:2. [9]John 14:13, 14. [10]Romans 8:26. [11]1 John 5:14. [12]1 Corinthians 14:16, 17.

22:4   Prayer is to be made for lawful things and for all kinds of people who are alive now or will live later.[13] But prayer should not be made for the dead[14] nor for those known to have sinned the sin that leads to death.[15]

[13]1 Timothy 2:1, 2; 2 Samuel 7:29. [14]2 Samuel 12:21–23. [15]1 John 5:16.

22:5   The elements of religious worship of God include reading the Scriptures,[16] preaching and hearing the Word of God,[17] teaching and admonishing one another in psalms, hymns and spiritual songs, singing with grace in our hearts to the Lord,[18] as well as the administration of baptism[19] and the Lord's supper.[20] They must be performed out of obedience to Him, with understanding, faith, reverence and godly fear. Also, purposeful acts of humbling[a] with fasting[21] and times of thanksgiving should be observed on special occasions in a holy and religious manner.[22]

[a]solemn humiliation. [16]1 Timothy 4:13. [17]2 Timothy 4:2; Luke 8:18. [18]Colossians 3:16; Ephesians 5:19. [19]Matthew 28:19, 20. [20]1 Corinthians 11:26. [21]Esther 4:16; Joel 2:12. [22]Exodus 15:1–19, Psalm 107.

22:6   Under the gospel, neither prayer nor any other part of religious worship is now restricted to or made more acceptable by the place where it is done or toward which it is directed. Instead, God is to be worshipped everywhere in spirit and in truth[23]—daily[24] in each family[25] and privately by each individual.[26] Also, more formal[b] worship is to be performed in public assemblies, and these must not be carelessly or deliberately neglected or forsaken, when God by His Word or providence calls us to them.[27]

[b]solemn. [23]John 4:21; Malachi 1:11; 1 Timothy 2:8. [24]Matthew 6:11; Psalm 55:17. [25]Acts 10:2. [26]Matthew 6:6. [27]Hebrews 10:25; Acts 2:42.

22:7   It is the law of nature that in general a portion of time speci-
       fied by God should be set apart for the worship of God. So
       by His Word, in a positive-moral and perpetual command-
       ment that obligates everyone in every age, He has specifically
       appointed one day in seven for a sabbath to be kept holy to
       Him.[28] From the beginning of the world to the resurrection of
       Christ the appointed day was the last day of the week. After
       the resurrection of Christ it was changed to the first day of the
       week, which is called the Lord's Day.[29] This day is to be kept to
       the end of the age as the Christian Sabbath, since the obser-
       vance of the last day of the week has been abolished.

[28]Exodus 20:8. [29]1 Corinthians 16:1, 2; Acts 20:7; Revelation 1:10.

22:8   The Sabbath is kept holy to the Lord when people have first
       prepared their hearts appropriately and arranged their every-
       day affairs in advance. Then they observe a holy rest all day
       from their own works, words and thoughts about their secular
       employment and recreation.[30] Not only that, but they also fill
       the whole time with public and private acts of worship and the
       duties of necessity and mercy.[31]

[30]Isaiah 58:13; Nehemiah 13:15–22. [31]Matthew 12:1–13.

XXIII
LAWFUL OATHS AND VOWS

23:1   A lawful oath is an element of religious worship in which a
       person swearing in truth, righteousness, and judgment sol-
       emnly calls God to witness what is sworn[1] and to judge the one
       swearing according to the truth or falsity of it.[2]

[1]Exodus 20:7; Deuteronomy 10:20; Jeremiah 4:2. [2]2 Chronicles 6:22, 23.

23:2   People should swear by the name of God alone and only with
       the utmost holy fear and reverence. Therefore to swear an
       empty or ill-advised oath by that glorious and awe-inspiring

name, or to swear at all by anything else, is sinful and to be abhorred.[3] Yet in weighty and significant matters, an oath is authorized by the Word of God to confirm truth and end all conflict.[4] So a lawful oath should be taken when it is required by legitimate authority in such circumstances.[5]

[3]Matthew 5:34, 37; James 5:12. [4]Hebrews 6:16; 2 Corinthians 1:23. [5]Nehemiah 13:25.

23:3   Whoever takes an oath authorized by the Word of God should consider with due gravity the seriousness of such a weighty act and to affirm nothing in it except what one knows to be true. For the Lord is provoked by ill-advised, false, and empty oaths, and because of them this land mourns.[6]

[6]Leviticus 19:12; Jeremiah 23:10.

23:4   An oath is to be expressed in the plain and ordinary meaning of the words, without any ambiguity or mental reservation.[7]

[7]Psalm 24:4.

23:5   A vow must not be made to any creature but to God alone. Vows should be made and performed with the most conscientious care and faithfulness.[8] However, Roman Catholic monastical vows of perpetual single life,[9] professed poverty,[10] and obedience to monastic rules, are by no means steps to higher perfection. Instead, they are superstitious and sinful snares in which Christians may not entangle themselves.[11]

[8]Psalm 76:11; Genesis 28:20–22. [9]1 Corinthians 7:2, 9. [10]Ephesians 4:28. [11]Matthew 19:11.

XXIV
CIVIL GOVERNMENT

24:1   God, the supreme Lord and King of the whole world, has ordained civil authorities to be under Him and over the people, for His own glory and the public good. For this purpose He has armed them with the power of the sword, to defend and encourage those who do good and to punish evildoers.[1]

[1]Romans 13:1–4.

24:2   Christians may lawfully accept and carry out the duties of public office when called to do so. In performing their office they must especially maintain justice and peace,[2] according to the wholesome laws of each kingdom or other political entity. To carry out these duties they are authorized now under the New Testament to wage war in just and necessary situations.[3]

[2]2 Samuel 23:3; Psalm 82:3, 4. [3]Luke 3:14.

24:3   Because civil authorities are established by God for the purposes stated, we should submit in the Lord to them in everything lawful that they require. We should submit not only for fear of punishment but also for the sake of conscience.[4] We ought to make requests and prayers for kings and everyone in authority, so that under their rule we may live a quiet and peaceful life in all godliness and honesty.[5]

[4]Romans 13:5–7; 1 Peter 2:17. [5]1 Timothy 2:1, 2.

XXV

MARRIAGE

25:1   Marriage is to be between one man and one woman. A man must not have more than one wife nor a woman more than one husband at the same time.[1]

[1]Genesis 2:24; Malachi 2:15; Matthew 19:5, 6.

25:2   Marriage was ordained for the mutual help of husband and wife,[2] for the increase of humanity with legitimate offspring,[3] and for the prevention of immorality.[4]

[2]Genesis 2:18. [3]Genesis 1:28. [4]1 Corinthians 7:2, 9.

25:3 Everyone who is able to give rational consent may marry.[5] Yet Christians are to marry in the Lord.[6] Therefore, those who profess the true religion should not marry unbelievers or idolaters. Nor should the godly be unequally yoked by marrying those who lead evil lives or hold to damnable heresy.[7]

[5]Hebrews 13:4; 1 Timothy 4:3. [6]1 Corinthians 7:39. [7]Nehemiah 13:25–27.

25:4 Marriage should not occur within the degrees of blood relationship or kinship that are forbidden in the Word.[8] These incestuous marriages can never be made lawful, so that the individuals may live together as husband and wife, by any human law or consent of the parties involved.[9]

[8]Leviticus 18. [9]Mark 6:18; 1 Corinthians 5:1.

XXVI

THE CHURCH

26:1 The catholic—that is, universal—church may be called invisible with respect to the internal work of the Spirit and truth of grace. It consists of the full number of the elect who have been, are, or will be gathered into one under Christ her head. The church is the spouse, the body, the fullness of Him who fills all in all.[1]

[1]Hebrews 12:23; Colossians 1:18; Ephesians 1:10, 22, 23; Ephesians 5:23, 27, 32.

26:2 All people throughout the world who profess the faith of the gospel and obedience to God through Christ in keeping with the gospel are and may be called visible saints,[2] as long as they do not destroy their own profession by any foundational errors or unholy living. All local[a] congregations ought to be made up of these.[3]

[a]*particular*. [2]1 Corinthians 1:2; Acts 11:26. [3]Romans 1:7; Ephesians 1:20–22.

26:3   The purest churches under heaven are subject to mixture and error.[4] Some have degenerated so much that they have ceased to be churches of Christ and have become synagogues of Satan.[5] Nevertheless, Christ always has had and will have in this world to the very end a kingdom of those who believe in Him and profess His name.[6]

[4]1 Corinthians 5; Revelation 2 and 3. [5]Revelation 18:2; 2 Thessalonians 2:11, 12. [6]Matthew 16:18; Psalm 72:17; Psalm 102:28; Revelation 12:17.

26:4   The Lord Jesus Christ is the head of the church. By the Father's appointment, all authority is conferred on Him in a supreme and sovereign manner to call, institute, order and govern the church.[7] The Pope of Roman Catholicism cannot in any sense be head of the church; rather, he is the antichrist, the man of lawlessness, and the son of destruction, who exalts himself in the church against Christ and all that is called God. The Lord will destroy him with the brightness of His coming.[8]

[7]Colossians 1:18; Matthew 28:18–20; Ephesians 4:11, 12. [8]2 Thessalonians 2:2–9.

26:5   In exercising the authority entrusted to Him, the Lord Jesus, through the ministry of His Word, by His Spirit, calls to Himself out of the world those who are given to Him by His Father.[9] They are called so that they will live before Him in all the ways of obedience that He prescribes for them in His Word.[10] Those who are called He commands to live together in local[a] societies, or churches, for their mutual edification and the fitting conduct of public worship that He requires of them while they are in the world.[11]

[a]particular. [9]John 10:16; John 12:32. [10]Matthew 28:20. [11]Matthew 18:15–20.

26:6   The members of these churches are saints by calling, visibly displaying and demonstrating in and by their profession and life their obedience to the call of Christ.[12] They willingly agree to live together according to Christ's instructions, giving themselves to the Lord and to one another by the will of God, with the stated purpose of following the ordinances of the gospel.[13]

[12]Romans. 1:7; 1 Corinthians 1:2. [13]Acts 2:41, 42; Acts 5:13, 14;
2 Corinthians 9:13.

26:7 To every church gathered in this way, conforming to Christ's
      mind as declared in His Word, He has given all power and
      authority that is in any way necessary to conduct the form
      of worship and discipline that He has instituted for them to
      observe. He has also given them commands and rules, to use
      and carry out that power rightly and properly.[14]

[14]Matthew 18:17, 18; 1 Corinthians 5:4, 5, 13; 2 Corinthians 2:6–8.

26:8 A local church, gathered and fully organized according to the
      mind of Christ, consists of officers and members. The offi-
      cers appointed by Christ are overseers or elders, and deacons.
      They are to be chosen and set apart by the church called and
      gathered in this way, for the distinctive purpose of admin-
      istering ordinances and for carrying out any other power or
      duty Christ entrusts them with or calls them to. This pattern
      is to be continued to the end of the age.[15]

[15]Acts 20:17, 28; Philippians 1:1.

26:9 Christ has appointed the way to call someone prepared and
      gifted by the Holy Spirit to the office of overseer or elder in
      a church. He must be chosen by the collective vote of the
      church itself.[16] He must then be solemnly set apart by fasting
      and prayer. The body of elders of the church must lay hands
      on him if there are any already in place.[17] A deacon must be
      chosen by the same kind of vote and set apart by prayer and
      laying on of hands as well.[18]

[16]Acts 14:23. [17]1 Timothy 4:14. [18]Acts 6:3, 5, 6.

26:10 The work of pastors is to give constant attention to the service
      of Christ in His churches in the ministry of the Word and
      prayer. They are to watch over the souls of church members
      as those who must give an account to Christ.[19] The church-
      es to whom they minister must not only give them all due
      respect but also must share with them from all their good
      things according to their ability.[20] They must do this so their

pastors may have a comfortable living without having to be entangled in secular matters[21] and so they can show hospitality to others.[22] This is required by the law of nature and by the explicit command of our Lord Jesus, who has ordained that those who preach the gospel should earn their living by the gospel.[23]

[19]Acts 6:4; Hebrews 13:17. [20]1 Timothy 5:17, 18; Galatians 6:6, 7. [21]2 Timothy 2:4. [22]1 Timothy 3:2. [23]1 Corinthians 9:6–14.

26:11   Although overseers or pastors of churches must be engaged in preaching the Word as a function of their office, yet the work of preaching the Word is not totally restricted to them. Others who are also gifted and prepared by the Holy Spirit for it and approved and called by the church may and should preach.[24]

[24]Acts 11:19–21; 1 Peter 4:10, 11.

26:12   All believers are obligated to join themselves to local[a] churches when and where they have the opportunity. Likewise, all who are admitted to the privileges of a church are also subject to the discipline[b] and government of it, according to the rule of Christ.[25]

[a]particular. [b]censures. [25]1 Thessalonians 5:14; 2 Thessalonians 3:6, 14, 15.

26:13   Church members who have been offended and have performed their duty concerning the person by which they are offended, should not disrupt any church action or absent themselves from the assemblies of the church or administration of any ordinances because of the offence at any of their fellow members. Instead, they should look to Christ in the further action of the church.[26]

[26]Matthew 18:15–17; Ephesians 4:2, 3.

26:14   Every church and all its members are obligated to pray continually for the good and prosperity of all churches of Christ in every place.[27] They must also—at every opportunity within the limits of their stations and callings—exercise their gifts and graces to benefit every church. Also, when churches are raised up by the providence of God, insofar as they enjoy opportunity and favorable circumstances for it, they should have fellowship[c] among themselves for their peace, growth in love, and mutual edification.[28]

[c]*communion*, implying formal association. [27]Ephesians 6:18; Psalm 122:6. [28]Romans 16:1, 2; 3 John 8–10.

26:15 Cases of difficulties or differences—doctrinal or administrative—may arise, touching on the peace, union, and edification of all churches in general or an individual church. Other cases may occur when a member or members of a church are injured in or by disciplinary action that is not in keeping with truth and order. In such cases, it is according to the mind of Christ for many churches having fellowship[c] together to meet through their messengers to consider and give their advice concerning the issue in dispute and to report their advice to all the churches concerned.[29] Nevertheless, these assembled messengers are not entrusted with any church authority, strictly speaking. Neither do they have any jurisdiction over the churches themselves, to exercise any discipline either over any churches or individuals or to impose their decision on the churches or officers.[30]

[c]*communion*, implying formal association. [29]Acts 15:2, 4, 6, 22, 23, 25. [30]2 Corinthians 1:24; 1 John 4:1.

XXVII
COMMUNION OF SAINTS

27:1 All saints are united to Jesus Christ their head by His Spirit and by faith, although this does not make them one person with Him. They have fellowship in His graces, sufferings, death, resurrection and glory.[1] Since they are united to one another in love, they have communion in each other's gifts and graces[2] and are obligated to carry out these duties, both public and private, in an orderly way to promote their mutual good, both in the inner and outer aspects of their lives.[3]

[1]1 John 1:3; John 1:16; Philippians 3:10; Romans 6:5, 6. [2]Ephesians 4:15, 16; 1 Corinthians 12:7; 1 Corinthians 3:21–23. [3]1 Thessalonians 5:11, 14; Romans 1:12; 1 John 3:17, 18; Galatians 6:10.

27:2   Saints by profession are obligated to maintain a holy fellowship and communion in worshiping God and in performing other spiritual services that promote their mutual edification.[4] They are to aid each other in material things according to their various abilities and needs.[5] They should especially exercise communion in the relationships they have in their families[6] and churches.[7] Yet the rule of the gospel also directs them, as God provides opportunity, to extend their sharing to the whole household of faith, to all those who in every place call upon the name of the Lord Jesus. Nevertheless, their communion with one another as saints does not take away or infringe on the title or individual ownership that people have in their goods and possessions.[8]

[4]Hebrews 10:24, 25; Hebrews 3:12, 13. [5]Acts 11:29, 30. [6]Ephesians 6:4. [7]1 Corinthians 12:14–27. [8]Acts 5:4; Ephesians 4:28.

XXVIII
BAPTISM AND THE LORD'S SUPPER

28:1   Baptism and the Lord's Supper are ordinances of positive and sovereign institution. They are appointed by the Lord Jesus the only lawgiver and are to be continued in His church to the end of the age.[1]

[1]Matthew 28:19, 20; 1 Corinthians 11:26.

28:2   These holy appointments are to be administered only by those who are qualified and called to administer them, according to the commission of Christ.[2]

[2]Matthew 28:19; 1 Corinthians 4:1.

XXIX
BAPTISM

29:1 Baptism is an ordinance of the New Testament, ordained by Jesus Christ. To those baptized it is a sign of their fellowship with Him in His death and resurrection, of their being grafted into Him,[1] of remission of sins,[2] and of submitting themselves to God through Jesus Christ to live and walk in newness of life.[3]

[1]Romans 6:3–5; Colossians 2:12; Galatians 3:27. [2]Mark 1:4; Acts 22:16.
[3]Romans 6:4.

29:2 Those who personally profess repentance toward God and faith in and obedience to our Lord Jesus Christ are the only proper subjects of this ordinance.[4]

[4]Mark 16:16; Acts 8:36, 37; Acts 2:41; Acts 8:12; Acts 18:8.

29:3 The outward element to be used in this ordinance is water, in which the individual is to be baptized in the name of the Father, and of the Son, and of the Holy Spirit.[5]

[5]Matthew 28:19, 20; Acts 8:38.

29:4 Immersion, or dipping of the person in water, is necessary for this ordinance to be administered properly.[6]

[6]Matthew 3:16; John 3:23.

XXX
THE LORD'S SUPPER

30:1 The supper of the Lord Jesus was instituted by Him the same night He was betrayed. It is to be observed in His churches to the end of the age as a perpetual remembrance and display of the sacrifice of Himself in His death.[1] It is given for the confirmation of the faith of believers in all the benefits of Christ's death, their spiritual nourishment and growth in Him, and their further engagement in and to all the duties they owe Him. The supper is to be a bond and pledge of their communion with Christ and each other.[2]

[1] 1 Corinthians 11:23-26. [2] 1 Corinthians 10:16, 17, 21.

30:2 In this ordinance Christ is not offered up to His Father, nor is any real sacrifice made at all for remission of sin of the living or the dead. It is only a memorial of the one offering Christ made of Himself on the cross once for all.[3] It is also a spiritual offering of the highest possible praise to God for that sacrifice.[4] Thus, the Roman Catholic sacrifice of the mass (as they call it) is utterly detestable and detracts from Christ's own sacrifice, which is the only propitiation for all the sins of the elect.

[3] Hebrews 9:25, 26, 28. [4] 1 Corinthians 11:24; Matthew 26:26, 27.

30:3 In this ordinance the Lord Jesus has appointed His ministers to pray and to bless the elements of bread and wine and in this way to set them apart from a common to a holy use. They are to take and break the bread, take the cup, and give both to the communicants while also participating themselves.[5]

[5] 1 Corinthians 11:23-26, etc.

30:4 Denying the cup to the people, worshipping the elements, lifting them up or carrying them around for adoration, or reserving them for some pretended religious use are all contrary to the nature of this ordinance and to the institution of Christ.[6]

[6] Matthew 26:26-28; 15:9; Exodus 20:4, 5.

30:5 The outward elements in this ordinance, properly set apart for the use ordained by Christ, have such a relationship to Christ crucified that they are sometimes called—truly though figuratively—by the names of the things they represent, that is, the body and blood of Christ.[7] However, in substance and nature they still remain truly and only bread and wine, as they were before.[8]

[7]1 Corinthians 11:27. [8]1 Corinthians 11:26–28.

30:6 The doctrine commonly called transubstantiation teaches that the substance of bread and wine is changed into the substance of Christ's body and blood by the consecration of a priest or some other way. This doctrine is hostile not only to Scripture[9] but also to common sense and reason. It destroys the nature of the ordinance and has been and is the cause of many kinds of superstitions and of gross idolatries.[10]

[9]Acts 3:21; Luke 14:6, 39. [10]1 Corinthians 11:24, 25.

30:7 Worthy recipients who outwardly partake of the visible elements in this ordinance also by faith inwardly receive and feed on Christ crucified and all the benefits of His death. They do so really and truly, yet not physically and bodily but spiritually. The body and blood of Christ are not present bodily or physically in the ordinance but spiritually to the faith of believers, just as the elements themselves are present to their outward senses.[11]

[11]1 Corinthians 10:16; 11:23–26.

30:8 All ignorant and ungodly people are unfit to enjoy communion with Christ and are thus unworthy of the Lord's Table. As long as they remain in this condition, they cannot partake of these holy mysteries or be admitted to the Lord's Table without committing a great sin against Christ.[12] All those who receive the supper unworthily are guilty of the body and blood of the Lord, eating and drinking judgment on themselves.[13]

[12]2 Corinthians 6:14, 15. [13]1 Corinthians 11:29; Matthew 7:6.

XXXI

THE STATE OF HUMANITY
AFTER DEATH AND THE
RESURRECTION OF THE DEAD

31:1   The bodies of those who have died return to dust and un-
        dergo destruction.[1] But their souls neither die nor sleep, be-
        cause they have an immortal character,[a] and immediately
        return to God who gave them.[2] The souls of the righteous
        are then made perfect in holiness and are received into par-
        adise. There they are with Christ and behold the face of God
        in light and glory while they wait for the full redemption of
        their bodies.[3] The souls of the wicked are thrown into hell,
        where they remain in torment and utter darkness, reserved
        for the judgment of the great day.[4] The Scripture recognizes
        no place other than these two for souls separated from their
        bodies.

    [a]*subsistence*; i.e., souls are not subject to dissolution. [1]Genesis 3:19;
    Acts 13:36. [2]Ecclesiastes 12:7. [3]Luke 23:43; 2 Corinthians 5:1, 6,8;
    Philippians 1:23; Hebrews 12:23. [4]Jude 6, 7; 1 Peter 3:19; Luke 16:23, 24.

31:2   At the last day, those saints who are found alive will not sleep
        but will be changed.[5] All the dead will be raised up with the
        very same bodies, not different ones,[6] though they will have
        different qualities. Their bodies will be united again to their
        souls forever.[7]

    [5]1 Corinthians 15:51, 52; 1 Thessalonians 4:17. [6]Job 19:26, 27. [7]1
    Corinthians 15:42, 43.

31:3   The bodies of the unjust will be raised by the power of Christ
        to dishonor. By His Spirit the bodies of the just will be raised
        to honor and will be made like Christ's own glorious body.[8]

    [8]Acts 24:15; John 5:28, 29; Philippians 3:21.

XXXII
THE LAST JUDGMENT

32:1 God has appointed a day in which He will judge the world in righteousness by Jesus Christ,[1] to whom all power and judgment is given by the Father. In that day, the apostate angels will be judged.[2] So also, all people who have lived on the earth will appear before the judgment seat of Christ, to give an account of their thoughts, words, and deeds and to receive a reckoning according to what they have done in the body, whether good or evil.[3]

[1]Acts 17:31; John 5:22, 27. [2]1 Corinthians 6:3; Jude 6. [3]2 Corinthians 5:10; Ecclesiastes 12:14; Matthew 12:36; Romans 14:10, 12; Matthew 25:32–46.

32:2 God's purpose for appointing this day is to manifest the glory of His mercy in the eternal salvation of the elect, and of His justice in the eternal damnation of the reprobate, who are wicked and disobedient.[4] For at that time the righteous will go into everlasting life and receive fullness of joy and glory with everlasting rewards in the presence of the Lord. But the wicked, who do not know God and do not obey the gospel of Jesus Christ, will be thrown into everlasting torments[5] and punished with everlasting destruction, away from the presence of the Lord and from the glory of His power.[6]

[4]Romans 9:22, 23. [5]Matthew 25:21, 34; 2 Timothy 4:8. [6]Matthew 25:46; Mark 9:48; 2 Thessalonians 1:7–10.

32:3 Christ desires that we be firmly convinced that a day of judgment will come, both to deter everyone from sin[7] and to comfort the godly more fully in their adversity.[8] For this reason, He has determined to keep the day secret, to encourage people to shake off any fleshly security and always to be watchful, because they do not know the hour when the

Lord will come[9] and so that they may always be prepared to say, "Come Lord Jesus; come quickly. Amen."[10]

[7]2 Corinthians 5:10, 11. [8]2 Thessalonians 1:5–7. [9]Mark 13:35–37; Luke 12:35, 36. [10]Revelation 22:20.

CPSIA information can be obtained at www.ICGtesting.com
Printed in the USA
LVOW081259140113

315631LV00002B/6/P